To my mother, Ormie Martin

My best example of a "1st Class" godly woman

1st *CLASS SINGLE*

RULES FOR DATING AND WAITING GOD'S WAY

Cheryl Martin

1st Class Single
by Cheryl Martin

Printed in the United States of America

Library of Congress Control Number: 2003100337
ISBN 1-591605-69-5

Xulon Press
www.XulonPress.com

Xulon Press books are available in bookstores everywhere, and on the Web at www.XulonPress.com.

P.29 Thought!
P51 sad, but true
P.110 ☆
P. 117
P.118 good assignment
P.128

Contents

Introduction

I don't need to tell you that there are a lot of single people in the world today. The singles population is booming in society and in the church. Many have never married and others are single again because of the high divorce rate or the death of a spouse. I would venture to say that most are single *not* by choice, but by circumstances beyond their control.

Chances are, countless Christian women are waiting and waiting and waiting and praying and praying and praying and asking God: "Lord, when will it be *my* time? I've dedicated my life to You; I'm living *all* I know how, and nothing is happening! I know You can work miracles, because there is nothing too hard for You. I'm not asking for much. One man will do; that's all I need. Just one, as a special delivery package from You!"

But year after year, the prayer goes unanswered. It can be disappointing at times. The "right" man just hasn't come along; or you thought he had, but he didn't see himself as your package! You long for marriage, but you can't get married by yourself. It takes two to make a relationship, and two to get married and stay married.

A minister and relationship expert, Louis Greenup, often tells the story of sitting in 1st Class during a flight one day and reflecting on the superior level of service in that section. The seats are roomier, the flight attendants are more attentive (providing hot towels and hanging up your coat), and choice meals are served on china. Everybody is on the same plane and will arrive at the same time to the same destination, but the service is superior in 1st Class. Greenup says the Lord spoke to him during one such flight and said, "I want you to have a 1st Class Marriage!" He went home and immediately focused on how he could provide his wife "1st class service" by doing things that would exceed her expectations and bring her great delight.

Every time I hear Louis Greenup tell that story, I say to God in my heart: "Lord, just as you wanted Greenup to have a 1st Class Marriage, I want to be a 1st Class Single! I don't want to be mediocre in any area of my life. I know I'm a Christian and I'm going to heaven because of my faith in You, but I want to arrive at the destination having lived a life of distinction that would bring You the highest praise. I want to fulfill my God-given purpose and fully embrace every season of my life. I confess, I want a man. A good man. A godly man, if that is Your will for me, but in the meantime I want to be exceptional in my single status."

I began to ask what would a 1st Class Single look like, when it comes to the choices made in dating and waiting? I realized this person would first go to the source of true wisdom, God, in order to make wise dating decisions. The Bible says, "For the Lord gives wisdom, and from his mouth come knowledge and understanding. For wisdom will enter your heart, and knowledge will be pleasant to your soul, discretion will protect you, and understanding will guard you" (Proverbs 2:6, 10-11).

To make the most of our season of dating, waiting, and desiring a mate, we women need authentic wisdom, knowledge, understanding, and discernment from God, the ultimate matchmaker. After all, love, marriage, and sex were His idea, not ours. (We weren't creative enough to dream up sex!)

Many Christian women don't have the right data when they start dating. (I know I didn't.) We make our best decisions when we take the time to gather pertinent information. For instance, we typically don't buy a house or car or decide on a college unless we do research. If it's inadequate, we could end up disappointed with our choice. "Knowledge is power," as the adage goes. The more knowledge we have, the wiser our decisions. That works for relationships as well.

You may be one such woman who is unclear about what you should do while you wait on God to bring "Mr. Right" into your life. *1st Class Single* provides some answers for you based on the best guidebook around: The Bible. It also includes lessons God has taught me through His Word, my own experiences, and the experiences of other women and men.

I have spent most of my life dreaming, longing, and wishing for a fantastic, fulfilling relationship with a man that would lead to marriage. This secret obsession probably began in junior high school and mushroomed later in life. I would go into my fantasy world and conjure up an idyllic scenario, even sprinkling some "spiritual" scenes in the script. For instance, the man of my dreams was always godly and had eyes only for me. He was handsome, strong, smart, wise, and accepted me unconditionally. We would have this unbelievable relationship of walking in harmony. We would be equally committed to devoting our lives to the things of God until He called us to our heavenly home. I would be content, at peace, and fulfilled. The only thing is, it has never happened. No relationship has measured up to this fantasy. Is it because in reality, I was looking for "Jesus" in the flesh?

I became a Christ follower as a child. My desire has always been to please Him and to pursue His purposes for my life. Unfortunately, while growing up in the church, I received very little practical counsel on dating and waiting for a mate. I was not told what to look for in a man or how to behave, except to marry a Christian and not have sex before walking down the aisle. But there is so much more in between to consider. I've always wanted to get it right and do it His way, but I haven't always succeeded. At times, I've made stupid mistakes that I regret. So, my dating record is not flawless, but along the journey, I have learned much.

There is so much I know now that I wish I had

known when I finally accepted a marriage proposal fifteen years ago. I was smart, levelheaded, and wanted nothing more than God's perfect will in my life. I remained pure, and was willing to wait for His leading. However, three years into the marriage, my husband left God and me. No amount of prayer and pleading for reconciliation changed his mind. I was devastated and depressed. This was not the scenario I had bargained for or dreamed about, especially as a committed Christian. I could not believe this was happening to me. I thought such a "nightmare" only happened to people who don't know God or who don't have an intimate relationship with Him. Wrong! It can happen to anyone, because a solid, permanent marriage takes the commitment of two people.

But this book is not about my failed marriage. It is about a resolve I now have to help women develop a "1st Class" mentality in their attitudes, actions, and dating relationships and to become "armed" with knowledge to make wise decisions before they say "I do."

I grieve whenever I hear of another marital breakup, especially among Christians. I also ache when I hear of another Christian single engaging in sex before marriage.

I firmly believe Romans 8:28, which says, "All things work together for good to those who love God and to those who are called according to His purpose." My marriage and the heartbreak it caused led me to experience God's unconditional love in a new way. I received His emotional healing, reexamined my thinking, renewed my mind, and promised God and myself that I would be a 1st Class Single no matter what! The road to this new plateau in my life has been a journey of awakening.

1st Class Single is dedicated to imparting God's wisdom, knowledge, and understanding as these blessings relate to dating. My desire is that this book will encourage you to glorify God in your dating, and to trust Him with your love life. He is a God who can be trusted. *1st Class Single* offers practical advice regarding what to look for and how to respond in dating situations, and how to make the most of your singleness. I give you 30 rules. All 30 may not apply to you. Focus on the ones that do. This list is not exhaustive; neither does it take the place of your individual responsibility to seek God's will regarding your specific situation. These rules are merely guidelines and signposts that will help you make decisions based on true wisdom and not your emotions. By following them, you will honor God during your dating and waiting. I pray this book will be a blessing to you in your journey towards a 1st Class Marriage.

Rule #1:

Pursue God, Not a Guy!

Many women don't feel complete unless they have a man. What a woman yearns for is true, fulfilling and intense love, and unconditional acceptance in a relationship that will last forever. But most are looking in all the wrong places, at all the wrong men, for all the wrong reasons. That's why most women easily fall under the spell of a man and his "love talk." She melts. It can be all lies, but she melts anyway. She gives up sex in hopes of getting love. He gives "love talk" in hopes of getting sex. This game has been played for centuries.

For many women, their self-esteem is rooted in being desired by the opposite sex. That's why sometimes, out of fear and desperation, ANY man will do, even the wrong man with the "right" line! That happened to me once. I had recently experienced the death of a relationship. I was deeply hurt and wounded. My self-esteem was low. That can happen when you experience rejection. Then "Jim" came along. I realize now I would not have looked at him twice, if I had been in my right mind. But I was lonely and needed affirmation. "Jim" sensed that and moved in for the kill. He was saying all the right things, and moving at lightning speed. I was not attracted to him. He was not spiritually grounded. But all that mattered at that moment was that he was interested in me.

After a few weeks of dating, my "eyes" opened, especially when he did not respect my boundaries. I kept ducking and dodging his attempts to get close romantically. I finally got the courage to tell him it was over. A couple of days later while praying, I asked God, "Why and how did I ever get involved with 'Jim'?" He said: "I'm glad you asked. You were needy. You needed affirmation. You were lonely." Then Jesus spoke so softly: "Let me affirm you. Let me tell you how wonderful and lovely you are. I don't have a hidden agenda. I'm not giving you a line. If you let me affirm you, you won't be so quick to respond to any and every man who wants you because you are needy. You will be discriminating. You will be complete in me, and feel good about yourself, because of my love for you." I got the message.

Despite the lyrics of popular love songs, the only person who can produce the kind of love women want is Jesus. He is the only person who can meet that deep longing in your heart, and love you as you want to be loved. He is the only one with a perfect score in loving (He created the concept) and the only one who comes with this guarantee: "I will never leave you nor forsake you" (Heb. 13:5). Only He promises to love us with an everlasting love, warts and all. In fact, His love is so intense He died to prove it. Name another man whose love for a woman caused him to die on a cross for her. Now, that's some kind of loving!

Only Jesus promises to supply all our needs and desires. The Bible says, "My God shall supply all your needs according to his riches" (Phil. 4:19). If you notice, it did not say that a man will supply all your needs. So why do so many women expect a man to be "Superman," to be exactly like God? Why do women want men to read their minds, fulfill their dreams, and be the perfect companion? No man can do that! When you fantasize about that kind of relationship, you are setting yourself up for a big disappointment. You are seeking the impossible.

So was the Samaritan woman in John 4. She was desperately looking for wholeness and security in her relationships with men. How do I know? She had been married five times and was working on her 6th man. Jesus told her what she was looking for was a total sense of fulfillment and unconditional love—none of which could be found in men, but only in Him. He invited her to drink of His "water" and promised she would never thirst again. She would no longer look to men to give her what only Jesus could give. Drinking of Him would free her "to give" and not always seek "to get!"

God placed within women this intense desire to be loved. It is legitimate. We dream about the "perfect" love relationship. We watch the soap operas and love stories, and we read the romance novels, and then go in search of that perfect love. The reality is that God created us with this vacuum that only He can fill. He designed us for a relationship with Him first, before we experience the love of a man. It goes beyond an initial salvation experience. I'm talking about a connection that allows Jesus Christ to fill you spiritually with Him! He desires that we seek Him first, that we want Him more than anything else and that we make our No. 1 priority pursuing this love relationship. He wants us to love Him with all of our heart, soul, mind, and strength.

Our love for Christ should be so all consuming and passionate that it controls what we think; how we think; and how we view Him, others, and ourselves. Our love for Him should be so intense that we want nothing that would displease Him, only those things that bring Him joy. It should hurt us to hurt Him by our words, thoughts or actions. We trust His refusals, knowing that He only denies us what would hurt us, and that all His decisions are wrapped in love. We may not understand them, but we trust Him and His love for us. No desire should consume us more than our love for God.

If a woman does not cultivate a passionate love affair with Jesus, and instead seeks it in men, she can easily come across as needy. A man can spot a needy woman a mile away. It's like a big neon sign is on her forehead flashing "Needy, Needy," in bold bright colors! She comes across as desperate, anxious, and willing to please at any cost. She will do almost anything to have a relationship. She may worship being in a relationship with a man more than she worships God. But the God we serve is a jealous God. He wants no rival in our hearts for His affection.

I found this out the hard way shortly after I finished college. I met the man of my dreams (or so I thought). I remember the first time I laid eyes on him. He was wearing a blue leisure suit. I inquired about him. (He did not inquire about me. That should have been a sign, but more about that later.) He appeared to meet everything on my superficial list. He was a minister, good looking, intelligent and attended Ivy League colleges. I became consumed with him. He got in my spirit. He was on my mind when I went to bed. I dreamed about him. I thought of ways just to be in his presence. I just knew he was my "special delivery package" sent from God. He had to be! After all, I was one of God's "choice servants".

I was a virgin, committed to waiting for God's best. He looked like God's best to me! I tried to be around him, hoping he would just talk to me. Then, I had a great idea. Along with some girlfriends, I planned a party for singles. Who was at the top of the guest list? You guessed right. He was. He came to the party and was the perfect gentleman. I needed a ride home (which conveniently happened to be on his way home) and he offered to take me. I was in seventh heaven! He finally asked me for my phone number. Because of my fantasy, I convinced myself that God was working on my behalf. Shortly after that we began dating, but it lasted only about a month or so. When he ended the relationship, I was devastated but I refused to accept "no" for an answer. After all, I had mentally started making wedding plans. I thought, this was just a "trick of the enemy." The devil was trying to block my blessing!

I moved to Plan B and sought to be his friend instead, believing that it would turn to love at any minute, but it didn't. I wanted him to be "Mr. Right" so badly. I worked hard in that one-sided relationship for at least three years! I had determination, perseverance, and true grit. In other words, I was a glutton for punishment. Why? I was a needy woman with low self-esteem who desperately longed for this relationship that would fulfill my dreams. I wanted him. I could not accept the fact that he was not interested in me. Fortunately, by God's grace, I was never intimate with him or involved in petting, yet he was "in my spirit." Can you imagine the basket case I would have been, if I had been intimate? The painful longing I was experiencing was bad enough!

Finally, when I relocated to another state, and it was clear the relationship was going nowhere, except around in my mind, I cried out to God and asked Him: "Why? Why didn't this relationship work? What went wrong?" He answered with two revelations: First, this man was not His choice for me, and second, I idolized him.

I hadn't heard that word "idol," except in the Old Testament when the children of Israel set up graven images and worshipped them rather than the true and living God. I hadn't thought about idols in the 20th century. God said again: "You idolized him. You thought more about him than you did Me. You were consumed with him, not Me! You talked about him constantly to anyone who would listen!"

Anything or anyone we place above God is an idol. No one should have God's place in our lives. That's a no-no! It won't work. It's warped and destined to fail. This was a hard lesson for me to learn, but God must be numero uno!

How do you make sure you are pursuing God first and not a mate? How do you make sure He is always in your thoughts and on your mind? You spend quality time in His presence by talking to Him (praying) on a regular basis, throughout the day. Act the way you act when you're madly in love (or think you are). The man is always on your mind no matter how busy you are. Just the thought of him can bring a smile to your face. Every chance you get you talk on the phone, send cards or go on dates.

When you really love Jesus, you regularly read His love letter to you, the Bible. Communicating with a man once a week or once a month is not enough when you are really in love. Nor is it enough when you are in pursuit of God. To truly pursue Him, you must learn as much about God and His ways as you possibly can. Search the Scriptures, meditate on them, memorize the Word, talk to others about Him, and listen to others talk about Him. Don't make a decision without asking Him for direction and guidance.

David was not a perfect man, but he was described as a "man after God's own heart." In many of the Psalms, David was very transparent about his relationship with God. "Your love is ever before me," he said. "One thing I ask of the Lord, this is what I seek: that I may dwell in the house of the Lord all the days of my life, to gaze upon the beauty of the Lord and to seek him in his temple. O God you are my God, earnestly I seek you, my soul thirsts for you, my body longs for you … on my bed I remember you; I think of you through the watches of the night. My soul clings to you."[1] That's not a man's love talk to a woman in the wee hours of the morning. That's David talking to God who is love! He loved God first before he came to love a woman. His self-esteem was based on God's view of him, not his job, his family, or anyone else. His intimate relationship with God sustained him throughout the challenges and triumphs of his life.

By relishing in God's love for us and loving Him in return, we can replace our insecurities with His security and our perceived flaws with His acceptance. In His eyes, "we are fearfully and wonderfully made," a fragrance of beauty.

Having a healthy and satisfying relationship with God first will increase your attractiveness to a potential mate. Why? You will be more balanced and realistic in your expectations because your intense needs for fulfillment, security, and unconditional love are met through God. Someone once said, "It takes two good eggs to make an omelet. If one is rotten, the omelet is rotten!" Ideally, both the man and woman need to be emotionally whole and healed of baggage from past relationships before they come together. Cultivating an intimate love relationship with God takes work, but it's worth it, and it shows God that we are putting first things first!

Rule #2:

Commit to the Perfect Matchmaker Your Desire for a Mate

There is absolutely nothing wrong with telling God you want a man! It is also appropriate to ask God to grant you favor with the right man. Favor comes from God. He welcomes your requests. I don't care how much you like a man, if he doesn't like you, a relationship won't materialize. That's where favor comes in from The Matchmaker. If you are trusting Him to bring the right person at the right time, you can ask Him to give you favor with "Sam" if it's His will. Then you can wait quietly and see what God does without trying to help Him out or manipulate the situation. If "Sam" does not make a move towards you, you know he is not God's choice for you.

Now, whenever I meet a man who sparks my interest, rather than tell him how I feel, I talk to God first. I say a prayer something like this: "Lord, he seems like a nice guy and someone I would be interested in dating. I pray that if this relationship is of You, that You would put the desire in his heart to pursue me. If he doesn't, I'll know that this friendship is not Your will. I will in no way try to manipulate this relationship." This has worked every time without me saying a word to the guy. My feelings don't get hurt if the guy is not interested, because I see the hand of a sovereign God at work. Our Father only orchestrates the best for His children!

We are encouraged in the Scriptures to pray often about everything that concerns us. Don't let up. God never tires of our prayers. Remember the parable of the persistent widow and unjust judge in Luke 18? The judge feared neither God nor man. The widow kept coming to him with a plea for justice. He finally answered the lady's request, not because he liked her, but because of her persistence in petitioning him.

Be specific when you pray. You will be more prone to recognize the answer to that prayer. Tell God exactly what you desire in a mate, but trust His final judgment. As one of my brothers once prayed, "Lord you know what I need, but you also know what I like." Always leave the final results up to Him. He knows what we need better than we do. Pray not only for what you want, but also ask God if marriage is His perfect will for you. It may not be.

And if it isn't, think about how much time you could waste going after something that is not in line with the design He created for you before the foundation of the world.

It occurred to me a couple of years ago that the *only* reason a committed Christian should get married is because it is God's perfect plan; He ordained it and He willed it so. That's the only reason. Not because we are lonely or want sex without sinning. Not because we're tired of working or we want children, but only because God ordained the relationship for His glory and for His purposes, not our selfish desires! When we operate in this mindset, we will not settle for less than God's best and we will wait for it.

God's track record in the matchmaking department is the best one around. So, why not trust Him? He tailor-made Eve for Adam. He knew Adam needed a wife even before Adam knew he needed a wife. Adam was quite pleased when he laid eyes on the woman God created for him. Some people are matchmakers, but their matches are not always perfect. His are. It was God who led Abraham's servant to Rebekah for Isaac. It was for God's higher purposes to grant Esther favor with a king and to make her the next queen. Through her influence a nation was saved. It was not by accident that the widow Ruth, a foreigner, caught the eye of the wealthy landowner Boaz. Through their union came the lineage of David.

God always knows what He's doing. We may not know, but the Bible says, "As for God, his way is perfect" (Psalm 18:30). Be willing to wait as long as it takes for God's choice. It's all a matter of trust. Do you believe that the sovereign God, who does all things well, knows what you need, and when you need it? Or are you afraid you might miss God's man for you, unless you take matters into your own hands?

That kind of thinking indicates you don't trust God. It's that simple. It says you trust your judgment more than you trust the God who created a perfect world in six days! Imagine. He did not have to undo anything He did in those six days. He spoke and it came to be. He got it right the first time. Do you believe that at the right moment He can have you cross paths with His ideal man for you, when you least expect it?

When you truly believe that, you will learn to see God in "all things," not just some things, but All things! That includes every disappointment, every rejection, every delay. You can confidently and patiently wait on Him because you know and believe Psalm 84:11: "He will withhold no good thing from those who walk upright."

Rule #3:

Want God's Will, Not Your Way!

Be honest. Do you really want God's will more than you want your way when it comes to dating and desiring a mate? Don't answer too quickly. Think hard and long about it.

The most important decision we can make is to relinquish all and follow Christ. This command goes beyond salvation. That's the first step. Once we commit to Christ, our greatest desire should be to cooperate with His designs and blueprints for every aspect of our lives, including our love life. That's how Jesus, our perfect example, operated. He had a resolve to only say and do what would please His Father. He never did or wanted anything out of selfish motives. He did not waste one minute trying to manipulate the circumstances to work His own agenda. He did not have an agenda separate from the Father's.

Jesus says repeatedly in the Gospel of John: "My food is to do the will of Him who sent me and to finish His work; I seek not to please myself, but Him who sent me. I have come down from heaven not to do my will, but to do the will of Him who sent me; I do nothing on my own but speak just what the Father taught me, I am not seeking glory for myself. If I glorify myself, my glory means nothing."[1] If we follow His example and live by this creed, it will be easier to "let go" of a relationship after God has posted a huge stop sign.

I now utter this prayer often: that my desire for God's will in my life will be stronger than my own. Before I'm faced with a temptation, I say to God periodically: "I want your will more than I want my way. I want no man, job, house, car, or status, more than I want You and your perfect plan for me." This prayer is an exercise in renewing my mind and it forces me to think on a higher plane. I remind myself that my life is not about my selfish desires, but it's about what my heavenly Father wants. We must remember that God always has our best interest at heart. "He has our back." We must trust that He does.

Rule #4:

Don't Be Anxious to Marry

God gave women the strong desire for marriage. Most of us start dreaming of our wedding day and our "knight in shining armor" when we are little girls. This dream stays with us throughout our lives. Even when a woman has a successful career, she can still feel unfulfilled without a man in her life. This longing can cause her to pursue a relationship for the wrong reason. She deeply wants the state of marriage. Almost any man will do, if he seems interested in her. She will overlook warning signs of incompatibility and move full steam ahead because she wants a man.

To help prevent this from happening, ask yourself some hard questions. "Why do I want marriage so badly? Do I want matrimony at any cost? Am I so lonely and so needy that I'll take any man who resembles Mr. Right? Am I more in love with the *idea* of being married and having children? Or am I really in love with this person? Is it love or lust?" The answers may be painful, but the exercise will be helpful in determining what is fueling your desire for a relationship. Ask the Lord to show you what's really going on underneath the surface.

After breaking an engagement, I asked myself the following tough, revealing question: "Why was I willing to go down the aisle, knowing there were a lot of unanswered questions, knowing we lacked compatibility in many areas?" I did not like the answer. In all honesty, it boiled down to one thing. Not love, but change. Yes, plain and simple change. I was ready for a change in my life. I thought marriage would bring excitement. I was tired of my job and my surroundings. I wanted to live out my fantasy of being a writer and speaker and have my husband support me. This guy appeared to be my ticket to a charmed life.

Still, I had reservations because some things were troubling me about the relationship. For instance, we had problems communicating and I never felt as if he truly cherished me, but I was forging ahead, working my plan. After all, he was saved and committed to God.

It was only God who rescued me from what would have been an absolute disaster. I wanted marriage for my convenience. What did love have to do with it? What did God's will have to do with it?

Nothing. I prayed daily that God would make His will clear and not let me make a big mistake and marry this guy if it wasn't His idea. God knew my heart. I did want His will more than my way. He finally got through to me. Someone once said, "It is better to be single, than to wish you were." The Bible says, "Be anxious for nothing (no thing, no man, no job, no car), but in everything by prayer and supplication with thanksgiving, make your request known unto God" (Phil. 4:6).

We must make sure we are not operating out of fear and anxiety. Fear can consume us, for instance, if we look around the church and see just two available guys (or none at all). Neither one really interests us, but we are fearful, that if we don't pick one, nobody will ever pick us because the pickings are slim! Or we are afraid that if we don't like someone who likes us, we won't get another opportunity.

The truth is, there is always another bus coming. It could be the express, but you're trying to get on a local. Or that may be the last bus for that day, but tomorrow, another fleet of buses takes that route. This is where faith kicks in. Expand your mind. Your mate may not live in your town or be in your church. Stop putting limits on God! You can meet him on a plane, train, or automobile; in the grocery store; at a park; in the hospital; at work; at a museum or on vacation. You get the idea.

Surrender your desire to God, especially your desire for a mate. We can be so self-centered when it comes to pursuing a mate. It's typically all about what we want, rather than what God wants for us.

Being a Christ follower means we submit to His Lordship. He had the perfect plan for our lives before the foundation of the world. It's about yielding our rights, our feelings, and our desires to whatever is His pleasure. Jesus said the cost of discipleship is to "deny self, take up your cross daily and follow me" (Luke 9:23). If marriage is God's perfect will for you, rest assured, it's His job to bring about a Divine connection between you and Mr. Right. He knows where you are and where your future mate is, and He will deliver on time!

We should not long for what God has not given us. That's how Eve got in trouble in the Garden, longing for the one thing God denied her. How many of us are consumed with the one thing (marriage) God has yet to give us? We may have completed our education and secured a good job, but we can't make a man marry us. We are blessed in innumerable ways, but instead of counting our blessings, we count the one denial. We are fixated on our single state.

Stop being anxious to go down the aisle. Fully embrace where you are right now. It's about God, His perfect timing and His will. It's not about you.

Rule #5:

If a Man is Interested, He Will Pursue You!

God has built into a man a strong desire to be the initiator in relationships. That's part of his manhood. He wants to seize the challenge. The Bible says, "He who finds a wife finds what is good and receives favor from the Lord" (Prov. 18:22). It does not say, "she who goes looking!" A man loves the pursuit. Trust me. When he sees what he wants, he goes after it. If a man you adore is not pursuing you, he is not interested in you! Let's settle this once and for all. He is not shy. You do not intimidate him. He does not need your help. One of my brothers (who had a lot of experience dating) told me: "If a man is interested, no distance will stand in the way. But if he is not interested, you can live next door, and that's too far for him to go."

Now if you are determined to take the initiative, to approach a man with free tickets to a concert, Sunday dinner at your place or access to your new sports car, and he takes you up on all of the offers, but he's still not interested, then "W.I.I.F.M." is at play. (The same brother, Jerry, taught me this.) What does "W.I.I.F.M." stand for? "What's in it for me!" In other words, he's using you, and you are allowing him to do so! Does he only respond to your "freebies" and never suggests a date on his own where he pays? Do you call more than he does? Are you always the one planning the holiday get- togethers? Then face the facts: He is *not* interested!

I learned this the hard way. Remember the guy I told you about in Rule #1 with the blue leisure suit? Here are more details to fill in the blanks. When we started dating, I started doing all the work. I was always available and accommodating. What a fool I was! But I was just so grateful to be in this relationship and so happy that he had chosen me out of all the "fair maidens" of the church. I was already fantasizing about a wedding. A friend went with me to a bridal salon so I could try on dresses. Had he hinted it was going in that direction? No. Was I ahead of him and God? Yes. I wanted him and I convinced myself that this was God's will as well. After all, he was perfect for me and I for him. See how delusion works? We psyche ourselves into thinking something is God's will, because it's what we want.

If only I had known what I know now: Men

always pursue the women who catch their eye. This guy, several years later, met the woman of his dreams, pursued, and married her.

Rule #6:

Go Fishing in the Right Pond

Date only Christian men. Let me say it again, date only Christian men! Why? Every date is a potential mate, and it doesn't take long to capture our hearts. This policy creates a safeguard. I used to be more liberal on this one, but no more. I learned my lesson the hard way. If you say you want to marry a man committed to God, why are you entertaining the thought of dating a handsome heathen? So he's cute, with a good job, strong morals, and he's interested in you, and no Christian guys are asking you out. But he's lacking the main ingredient; he does not love God, but you do. He's not saved! It doesn't matter if he fits 49 items on your list of 50. If he is not walking with God, he is *not* Mr. Right.

Why tempt yourself?

Trust God and trust me on this one. The man may fill your void of loneliness, but God has not called you to engage in "missionary dating." It's not your job to lead him to the Lord in hopes God will lead both of you down the aisle. I know how it works. You start taking him to church, buying him all the sermon tapes, praying for his salvation, and putting him on everybody's prayer list, because you believe the Lord revealed to your spirit that this was the man for you! The only thing is, no one else is convinced he is.

Your priorities are mixed up. If you were honest with yourself, you would admit he is not the one, despite the fact that the relationship feels so good. Yes, you are happy and "in love," but you have overlooked God's basic principles. He does not need your help to save the man He has for you. I learned it is very difficult to tell whether a man who is interested in me suddenly starts pursuing God because he wants me or because he sincerely loves God.

Many men camouflage their true motives to get a "good Christian woman." Over the ages, many Christian women have succumbed to this mirage. They discovered only after they said, "I do" that the man did not truly make a life-changing commitment to follow Christ. It doesn't matter how long you've been walking with God; you are still vulnerable to such a deceptive, sincere-sounding man. Don't think you are strong enough to date unsaved men casually and maintain your objectivity. You are begging for trouble. If you never date a non-Christian, you never have to worry about falling in love and marrying one!

The Bible says, "Do not be unequally yoked with an unbeliever" (II Cor. 6:12). Make up your mind before the option is presented that you will not date a non-Christian. Why? Because you want God's best and a non-Christian boyfriend is not His best. God will honor your decision. The best barometer of someone's spirituality is his history *before* you met. What is his reputation? Is he known for pursuing God and seeking to please Him with his life choices? If so, these are signs that he was loving God before he met you.

Allow me to underscore my point: I'm not saying date a man because he is a Christian. I'm saying only date a man if he is a Christian. Other qualities matter as well, but this one is essential.

When someone wants to introduce you to a great guy, your first question should be: "Is he a committed Christian?" If the answer is no, then politely decline the introduction, no matter what else he has going for him. You know right away that he is not your God-ordained package! If, by a slight chance He is, God knows how to change his heart and save him without your help. Now that is really trusting God.

Rule #7:

Create a "Marriage Resume and Classified Ad"

This is another way of saying, know your non-negotiables and stick to them. If you go to the mall to buy a dress, you will be there all day if you don't have an idea of the kind of dress you're looking for, the color, and the price range. But if you know in advance, your search will go much faster. Know what you're looking for in a mate, and you can eliminate very quickly unqualified candidates. Psychologist and author Neil Clark Warren says, know your "must haves" and your "can't stands."[1]

While you're single, you should have a list. What are the absolute essentials you are looking for in a mate? What is your value system? What do you believe God is calling you to do, and what kind of mate would complement that calling? If you believe God wants you in full-time ministry, but the person you're dating has no interest in ministry and derides your calling, then that should tell you something. What are the things you cannot tolerate? If you must marry someone gainfully employed and you meet someone without a job (and he's not looking for one and hasn't worked in years), you don't need to go past a conversation. Case closed.

Your "can't stand" list may include someone who is verbally abusive, lazy, or who has children. The list is different for each person. God allows us to have preferences. After all, we all like different foods, cars, and clothing. That's OK. God likes diversity, but you need to know what you are about before you meet someone. What is it you can't live with? A dirty man? Someone who is jealous, or who uses profanity? Some women don't mind if the man is unemployed, as long as he's good looking and wants her. Whatever works for you.

The more you know your qualifications and expectations before you meet someone, the easier it will be to discern if this person is for you. Think about it. We use this procedure in other areas of our lives. When we decide to become homeowners, we go through a process of elimination: "Do I want a condominium, townhouse, or single family home? Do I want to live in the city or suburbs? Which neighborhood? What can I afford? Do I want a new house or an older one? Is a garage mandatory?"

If all these questions and others are decided beforehand, the search will be more productive. You can tell the realtor exactly what you're looking for. You would be upset if you told the agent you are interested only in single-family homes in a certain community at a certain price, yet every day she calls you up about a condo in an undesirable neighborhood. You would probably get another agent, because the person is not respecting your decision making and instead is trying to steer you in a direction you do not want to go.

But how many of us say we know what we want in a man, but we aren't willing to wait for it? We take any man who comes by, even if he's not what we've been praying for. We are just thrilled to have a man, any man! We need to be more discriminating and determined to wait for what God wants to give us. We usually live with regrets when we don't.

When I was looking for a home, I prayed specifically about what I wanted—the neighborhood, the price, everything. When the realtor showed me the place, I was excited, because it was exactly what I had prayed and asked God for. Now, there were some areas to negotiate, but I trusted God that if this was His will, He would work on my behalf. He did. I did not have to compromise on price or go beyond what I could afford to get my heart's desire. This works in relationships as well. God will never have you compromise His principles to get His best. Never!

Make sure that what is on your list of nonnegotiables is realistic and not superficial. In other words, don't make a list for the perfect man. Are you more concerned about his character or his clothes? His spiritual beliefs or his body? One time the Lord told me my list was very superficial. I was focusing on pedigree and looks, rather than "Does he have a heart for God? Is he kind? Faithful?" The Bible says, "Man looks at the outward appearance, but the Lord looks at the heart" (I Sam. 16:7). Looks will change, but a heart that longs for God reflects greater "beauty" over time.

Rule #8:

Develop the Qualities You Seek in a Mate

Many Christian women can recite a long list of what they are looking for in a potential mate. They want a Christian man who is smart, good looking, sensitive, and athletic with a good paying job and sense of humor. Now ask yourself, would such a together man be interested in dating you? Make sure you qualify for your own list! This is the time to be all you can be. I heard Pastor and author John MacArthur say, "A truly godly man wants a godly woman." A smart, self-motivated, disciplined person will probably be looking for someone of like mind. So, take that mate checklist of yours and get busy working on it *and* on you!

Have a vision of the kind of woman you want to be and the image you want to project. Keep it before you. Make a list of what you want to change about yourself and what you want to accomplish. Make it realistic. Seek input from friends. They may tell you to smile more, for instance, because your facial expressions don't make you look approachable. You may see the need to get out of your comfort zone and take a college course, travel abroad, or learn a new skill in order to increase your personal assets.

Rule #9:

Friendship First

Many women have one thing on their minds—getting the man to the altar. This preoccupation makes them forfeit the foundation of a good friendship. You say you love him, but do you <u>like</u> him? Can you share your heart with this man? Are you best friends? Do you share the same values? It is so important to develop the friendship component before you move to the next level.

The Bible says, "Above all else, guard your heart, for it is the wellspring of life" (Prov. 4:23). I've discovered that once a man has captured a woman's heart, it is almost impossible to change her mind about the relationship even though warning signs are everywhere. She possesses what I call a "glazed-over look." She is almost beyond the point of reason. Why? Because she wants him and loves him.

Pray constantly for God to help you guard your heart. Go slowly in the discovery phase of the friendship. Take it one step at a time. The heart is the seat of your emotions. Songs of Solomon says repeatedly that we should not awaken love until it's time. Often, we have not taken the time to know the man—really know him—and develop a friendship before we've fallen in love with him.

Friendships develop out of mutual respect. When a relationship is based on authentic friendship not lust, it has a much better chance of going the distance. Seek to build a solid foundation with an abiding friendship. That way, even if it does not progress to marriage, you will always have a friend.

Rule #10:

Seek God's Input from the Start

Pray about whether you should accept the first date. The answer could be "no," which will save you a lot of time and potential heartache. I wish someone had told me a long time ago to include God early in the equation. After all, He is willing and waiting to lead and guide us in the way we should go. No request is too small or trivial.

I love the story in the Old Testament of Abraham sending his trusted servant to find a wife for his beloved son, Isaac. Abraham had some nonnegotiables: She must come from his homeland and she could not be a foreigner. He also wanted her to have a godly heritage. He prayed, with high expectations, that God would go before his servant and guide him to the right woman for Isaac.

Once outside the city, the servant pleaded to God for success in his assignment. He prayed specifically that God's choice for Isaac would not only offer him a drink at the well, but also offer to give all his camels a drink! He was looking for this specific distinguishing mark of kindness. God honored his prayer. Before he finished praying, Rebekah appeared on the scene, and followed the script of his prayer. He asked her for a drink. She quickly complied and then offered to draw water for all his camels. This was no easy task. Camels consume a lot of water. But Rebekah did not complain. She exhibited an excellent attitude as she performed this act of kindness. The servant did not say anything, but watched her to confirm that God had answered his prayer.

When we seek God's input and our motives are pure, He often gives us more than we ask for. The servant was looking for specific internal qualities in Isaac's future wife: humility and kindness. He did not pray about her looks and shape. God took care of that on His own accord. As Genesis 24:16 says, "Now the young woman was very beautiful to behold, a virgin; no man had known her." She willingly left her homeland to marry Isaac without a picture or videotape presentation. When they met and married, verse 67 says, "Then Isaac brought her into his mother Sarah's tent; and he took Rebekah and she became his wife, and he loved her." What a difference it made in his life that God's input was sought before the search began.

I wish I had done this with a guy I was introduced

to by a dear friend. After talking with him for hours, she was convinced she had discovered the perfect mate for me. She couldn't wait to get home to tell me the news. She called me from her cell phone and said: "Girl, you won't believe it, but I have met your mate. I know it. I know it. I know it! You are going to be so happy, you are going to kiss my feet! I know that I just met your husband!"

Well, what do you do after your friend makes such a bold declaration? In hindsight, I now know exactly what you should do: remain calm, listen, still take the matter to God, and wait until you get an answer from Him before making a move. It's OK to listen to well-meaning friends, but you want to get your marching orders from God and God alone!

So what happened in my case? I talked to the guy. We had a pleasant conversation. We scheduled a date. I was a little skeptical about a blind date (I had been burned a couple of times) but I knew he was a Christian. I did pray on the way to the meeting place, not whether this was God's will, but that he would have the look I like. Now how superficial was that? Well, we met and that prayer was answered. He looked like my type. Amazing! For the first time on a blind date, here was a guy I would have been drawn to if I had seen him in a crowded room. (That's probably one of the reasons I stayed in the relationship as long as I did.)

We had a decent time, but I came home confused. The date, in my opinion, was unusual, not like the typical date where there is a natural flow of conversation from both parties. I called my mother and told her about it. The fact that I was expressing some concerns this early should have been a sign. But did I adhere to the sign? No. That leads me to the next point: Cut your losses early!

Rule #11:

Cut Your Losses Early

Be honest with yourself. You know something is wrong with the relationship. It's not clicking. Yes, you are both Christians, but you are not compatible. Don't play games. Don't kid yourself. Get out of it as fast as you can if you were hoping it would lead to marriage! Don't try to convince yourself that it's going to get better or that his best side simply has not emerged. As my mother has told me on several occasions, "Cheryl, that *is* his best side!" Don't languish because you're glad to be in a relationship, and you went dateless for years before this prospect came along. Now you're afraid that if you cut him loose, it will be another five-year drought! I know; I've been there. But I still say, cut your losses early.

I knew the guy I met on the blind date was not right for me, yet I dated him off and on for years! I kept waiting to see certain changes. I was "keeping hope alive." It was a waste of precious time that I could have spent being totally focused on the things of God. But I simply wanted it to work, so I kept trying to work it. After all, he had a lot of things going for him: he was a Christian, handsome, he had a good job, was financially secure, and had a good family background. But again, some major concerns stared me in the face and for a while I tried to ignore them. Don't make this mistake, ladies. You know deep in your heart when something is not right; you know 2 + 1 does not equal 4! Don't kid yourself. Cut your losses and move on with faith that God's best for you will be revealed.

Rule #12:

Look at the Signs ... then Wonder!

Investigate before you invest. You want to "see" as much as you can while dating, and "see" as little as you can after you get married. Unfortunately the reverse usually happens. We are blinded by love before marriage, and "see" too much after we say, "I do." Analyze *all* the data. Dating is the time to ask as many questions you can think of; to observe his character and personality; to find out about his family, his likes, dislikes, work ethic, and integrity; and to learn everything about him that's important to you. Does he read? What does he like to read? How does he spend his spare time? Does he want children? How does he view the wife's role? Typically, a woman can be so starry-eyed when dating that she sees only what she wants to "see," while overlooking chinks in the man's armor.

Take time while you're dating to stop, look and listen. Remember the childhood rule: "Stop, look and listen, before you cross the street?" Well, stop, look, and listen while dating. You should pause often, look at all the signs and signals, listen more than you talk and then wonder about the data. Don't ignore potential warning signs, especially red flags and yellow caution lights! For example: he gave you his pager, work and cell phone numbers, but not a home number. Why? Or he can't keep a job; he's had 10 jobs in two years! Why? He doesn't have a credit card. Don't assume it's because he doesn't believe in debt. It could be that his credit history is so bad, no company wants to take that risk. Or let's say he hit you in a fit of rage, you caught him in a lie, or he's intensely jealous. These are all signs.

You have three choices: ignore them, adjust your speed accordingly and slow down, or if necessary, take the exit ramp. When you get to a stop sign or red light, it's best to stop. Typically, we are guilty of ignoring these signs. We see them, we read them, but we think we can fix the man we desire and change the signs. Love conquers all, we say.

One of my brothers, a pastor, says that whenever he counsels a couple, and the wife points out some serious character flaws, patterns, or addictions, he will ask her privately whether she had any inkling before marriage that these problems existed. Inevitably, the wife always says, "Yes." Again, unfortunately, we "see" what we want to "see" before marriage.

I've never heard the testimony of a man treating his wife better after marriage. More often I hear stories of a great courtship, and now the wife wishes the marriage could be like that wonderful courtship. She closed her eyes to any incompatibility during courtship, but opened them wide after marriage. However, deep inside she always knew that those same problems, for instance, lying, laziness, and being inconsiderate, were there when they were dating. She just chose to overlook them. After marriage is the time to keep your eyes half closed to your spouse's imperfections. No one wants to be viewed as "a project" or "makeover." You made the choice. What you see is what you get.

But before you say, "I do," you still have time to back out. Always keep the back door open. Check out as much as you can. Does he have ring around the collar? If that's a pet peeve, check the collar. What about his hygiene? It could be a sign that cleanliness is not important to him. Is spending time with God a top priority for him? If not, then don't expect him to take the lead spiritually in your home. If these are not issues with you, fine. But if they are, take note and factor this information into your decision.

We can be so blinded by love or want marriage so desperately that we move full steam ahead, refusing to read the signs slowly and change course accordingly. The end results are not promising for those who overlook the warning signs.

Rule #13:

Ask God to Reveal Anything that is Hidden

The Bible says, "The lamp of the Lord searches the spirit of a man; it searches out his inmost being" (Prov. 20:27). "The Spirit searches all things, even the deep things of God" (I Cor. 2:10). So your man looks good, talks good, walks good, but what about his spirit, his true intentions? You don't know his heart, but God does. You don't know his real motives in pursuing a relationship with you, but God does. So, why not faithfully pray and ask God to search out your man's spirit? Whenever I've done this, it has worked every time. It has kept me out of hot water.

Now when I meet a man who's interested in dating me, I go to these scriptures, put his name there, along with the date I asked the Lord to search his heart. Each time I've been able to go back and record the day the prayer was answered. God loves when we include Him in our decision making.

Our knowledge is faulty at best. We need all the help we can in making one of the most important decisions of our lives. I remember meeting a man at a store. Once again, he looked like my type. We had an engaging conversation and I gave him my phone number. He started calling me. He sounded so spiritual. He claimed to be a deacon at his church. He was taking me pretty fast. I remember one Sunday afternoon lying across my bed and praying intensely for God's wisdom about this situation. I felt like something was not right about this "picture." There were some missing pieces to the puzzle.

I cried out to God and told Him my knowledge was limited and I needed His insight, discernment, wisdom and knowledge. "Please reveal to me 'Sam's' heart, and let me know anything that is not right," I cried. After a time of silence and waiting on God, He delivered. He made it very clear to me to get out of this friendship quickly, and walk away from it very gingerly, because this man had misrepresented himself. He was perpetrating! God also gave me a strategy for confirming my concerns and intuition. I am so thankful we serve a God who is willing to impart His divine wisdom to our situations in life. All we have to do is ask.

Rule #14:

Beware! Your Fantasies and Expectations Can Get You in Trouble

I've discovered that a woman has the amazing ability to believe what she wants to believe. She tends to fantasize about a relationship. She can think long and hard about it, and want it so badly that the next thing you know, she is convinced that this relationship is of God. She truly believes that the guy is madly in love with her and that the wedding is just around the corner. Chances are, he has only said "hello" with a smile or taken her on one date. With that, her mind is gone and she is twenty paces ahead of the guy. In reality, he has given her no reason to believe they have a future together. She is deceived by her delusion, easily dreaming about what their future could be, rather than focusing on what it is, which is usually nothing.

I've made the mistake of jumping to conclusions. There was a guy I admired from a distance. I thought he was distinguished looking. We would have brief conversations. He would simply say "hello," and that he enjoyed my talks at a singles group. That was it. I longed for us to have a longer conversation and to get to know each other. Finally, after speaking before a group, I got his attention and started a conversation. It went on and on. From my perspective, it was a delightful chat. My fantasizing pumped into high gear. Afterwards, I began to plan events where I could invite him. I was excited. The adrenaline was flowing. I saw great possibilities with this guy.

Then one morning when I was exercising, the Lord stopped me on the treadmill and said: "Cheryl, think about it, 'Carl' has not given you one legitimate indication he has any interest in you. All he did was talk to you once for a long time! He did not approach you first. In fact, he never approached you. He has not asked you for your phone number. He did not take the first or second step. So what makes you think he is interested in you? He has done nothing but respond when you initiated! So where are you getting this grand idea that you have a future with him?"

I was speechless! What could I say? God was right. I was wrong. I had gotten an idea and run with it! It was a relationship only in my mind. It never existed. "Carl" did not have a clue, and he was not interested. Sure enough, he never made a move, and I never made another one. I was relieved God stopped me from making a fool of myself! I was getting ready to forge full steam ahead based solely on my fantasies and false expectations.

Repeatedly, I've realized it is necessary to put all my dreams and fantasies on the altar of sacrifice. I need to part with them; to relinquish all my desires to the Lordship of Jesus Christ. This is a process. I did not realize how long I'd been living with these fantasies. I began to see that I had them since I was a child. I would go into my room and in silence fantasize about a perfect, loving relationship with a man. I told no one but God. As an adult, I thought I had given everything to God, had turned over every room and every corner of my heart, but I had not. Because this was a good, pure fantasy, I thought it was OK to keep it. Not so. Again, there must be *no* rival in our hearts for His affection, not even a colorful fantasy or holy desire. Only God's way is perfect! In the final analysis, "His ways are not our ways, neither His thoughts, our thoughts" (Isaiah 55:8).

I believe our ability to fantasize can be a blessing and a curse. A blessing, because we can see "through the eyes of faith" a brighter future. A curse, because we allow fantasy to blot out the real truth. And if we are not careful, we can be willing to make our dreams come true "at any cost." When we are consumed with our dreams and someone comes along who fits them, it is nearly impossible to extricate ourselves from him, because he fits our fantasy. This is a trick of the devil! We go after the object of our fantasy. We get him. We find out (usually when it's too late) that it was all a mirage.

Typically when we are obsessed with fantasies, we are willing to ignore wise counsel and warning signs, because we have a Burger King mentality and want to have it "our way." We justify our decisions by saying, this must be of God because "he" is the person of "my dreams." That's how I justified my decision to marry. During courtship, he and I prayed together, went to church together, studied the Bible together, even took our Bibles with us to the restaurant for Saturday breakfast. It was a God-honoring courtship from beginning to end. You can't get holier than that! How could this *not* be God? My courtship was *exactly* as I had dreamed. Any thoughts of potential warning signs contrary to this were pushed aside, because my fantasy was being fulfilled! I refused to see anything else. I had lost sight of a critical reality—that I should be consumed by His dreams, not mine.

In our dreams and fantasies, we always look good. We are always happy. Life is perfect. But God is about orchestrating situations and circumstances that will achieve His purposes and conform us into His image. In other words, He's fitting us for heaven! God's plans for our lives are always totally different from what we can imagine. That's why He is God, and we are not. Our thinking is absolutely minuscule, a thimble's worth (and that may be too generous) compared with the omnipotence and omniscience of God!

Consider the example of Mary. The mother of

Jesus relinquished her dreams once she heard from the angel that God had great plans for her. She was engaged and planning her wedding to Joseph. God had another idea, a grander idea. He had earmarked Mary to be the mother of the Son of God! The Holy Spirit would impregnate her. This news undoubtedly interrupted her plans. Mary's response? In Luke 1:38, she answered, "I am the Lord's servant. May it be to me as you have said."

It is a wise decision to cling to Him not to your dreams and fantasies. You should offer your desires to Him and say: "Do with me what You will. You are the Master. I am the servant. You are the potter. I am the clay. Your way is always best."

This probably won't be a one-time exercise. Our dreams and fantasies can be bondage, a stronghold in our lives. Long-term habits don't want to die. They will reappear when you least expect. Don't be surprised or dejected when they do. Just continually bring them back to the foot of the Cross and leave them there. The Bible tells us to "cast down vain imaginations" (II Cor. 10:5). In other words, we are to go only with the facts! Be honest with God. Tell Him that you are still struggling with relinquishing your dreams of a particular mate or job. I've had to do that. He knows our frailties. He understands. He will help us.

I know it's difficult, but try very hard (by God's grace) not to fantasize about a current relationship or future relationship. Train your mind to take it one step at a time. Pray and ask the Lord for His help. Don't assume that a man is interested in you simply because he is nice to you or offers to help or pray for you. Don't assume anything. Try to stop the habit of "writing the script" before any action has taken place.

Ask God to reveal His vision for you and His purpose. He may reveal that your dream is not His dream for you; it may be His will but it's not His time, or God may grant you the desires of your heart, and when He does you will not be anxious, and the desire will not be an idol. You can handle it.

Remember when God tested Abraham by asking him to sacrifice what he loved most, his only son, Isaac? God had given him Isaac in his old age. He did this to fulfill His promise to Abraham. But then God asked Abraham to sacrifice Isaac on the altar. It was only a test (but Abraham did not know it at the time). God wanted to make sure Abraham did not love the gift more than the giver. He did not. Obedience to God was more important.

Do you want the gift of marriage or the gift of a relationship more than the giver of every good and perfect gift? If so, you are setting yourself up for failure.

It is important to note that our fantasies and expectations can get us in trouble in other areas of our lives, not just in courtship. I remember when I used to constantly desire to host my own television show. I was patient most of the time, trusting the Lord. But occasionally in my career, I was anxious and felt a sense of entitlement that I deserved my own show. I never verbalized this, but I certainly thought it.

God began to deal with my attitude. There was a chance to host a new show and I auditioned and got the co-host slot. Initially I was excited, but there were certain warning signs that this opportunity was not right for me. First of all, the executive producer did not want me as the host. Also, I would have to spend most of my Sundays taping the program. In addition, I would not get a pay increase, but instead work a six-day week!

At first, I was willing to overlook all of this because I wanted to host a show. Despite all the confusion, I was still moving forward until the Lord spoke quietly to my heart after church service one Sunday. He said: "Cheryl, let it go. There is too much confusion. This is not My will for you. It is more important to Me that you spend time on Sundays in worship with other believers. Your soul needs that."

Calmness immediately came over me. I knew I had heard from God. He is not the author of confusion. I was fighting an uphill battle. I wrote a letter the following day stating that I was passing on the opportunity and I explained why. I never regretted the decision.

Obeying God in this instance led to greater opportunities. Less than a year later, I was a contender to host one of two shows. During the waiting period, I committed my desires to the Lord and said: "Lord, I want Your will, more than I want my way. I'm trusting that Your perfect will be done, even if it means I don't get to host any show. I leave it in Your hands. What is most important is being in Your will. I leave the results to You."

I was no longer anxious about hosting a television show. My ego was not involved. There was no sense of entitlement. As it turned out, I was selected to host a unique news analysis program that I had never dreamed about. I knew that God had selected the best opportunity for me. Because I had given my desires to Him, God gave me what He deemed best. Every day I recognized that my job was an example of His mercy and grace, and I was there to bring glory to Him. He made it possible.

When we die to self, God can work His plan. He will always give us what we need, not necessarily what we want. But it will always be His Best for us. So make room for Him to work in your life by moving your agenda aside.

Rule #15:

Don't Try to Make, Force, or Buy a Relationship

How many times have you tried to **make** a guy like you? Be honest. How many times have you tried to **force** a relationship? Remember when you were the one doing all the work? You always called first, had the ideas for dates, and were even willing to pay, just to be in his company? It still did not work out, did it?

Some women have been so desperate for a guy to like them that they shower him with expensive gifts. In return, they get nothing but the bill, heartache and exhaustion. Yet, they still hang on. They have tried everything they could. Remember, if it's too much work, it is too much work, especially if you're the only one doing the work.

The will of God is *never* forced! Why would God put you in the position where you must work hard to convince a man that you're the one, the only one for him? The answer is, He wouldn't! Unfortunately, your actions reveal your desperation and insecurity. I've been in relationships where I was working too hard; in fact, I was doing all the work. I was always the one doing the accommodating. I never expressed my disappointment. Why? I was just glad to be dating the guy. I was so honored and grateful he was interested in me! If he disrespected me, I would not say anything. If he arrived 45 minutes late for a date, I would suppress my frustration, because I so wanted the relationship and I did not want to do anything to "rock the boat."

I did not realize that I did not respect myself. Others don't respect you when you don't respect yourself. All of my accommodating did not endear this guy to me. In fact, my anxieties and insecurities probably contributed to the demise of the relationship. I allowed him to walk all over me. And I kept coming back for more. When a relationship is right and of God, you will *not* have to make, force, or buy it!

Rule #16:

Don't Have Sex!

I know that according to all the latest music and videos, everybody's doing it and you can't live without sex because your hormones never stop "moaning!" That's a lie! A 1st Class Single seeks to honor God by remaining pure and setting boundaries before she goes on the first date! It's important to know your hot buttons, what turns you on to the point of no return.

I grieve every time I hear stories of Christian singles engaging in sex. Why? It says to unbelievers that our standards in dating are no different than theirs and while we have trusted God for salvation, we have not trusted Him fully to manage our love life.

A 1st Class Single will realize God's restrictions are for her own good. He designed the ultimate gratification of sex to be experienced only in the context of a loving, committed relationship between a husband and wife. One man. One woman. He did not want women to be taken advantage of by multiple sexual partners or by men who only want their bodies, but not them. He did not provide the gift of sex for women to experience emotional scars, abuse, and rejection. But so many women have lasting pain because they have not been discriminating. They have refused to "play by God's rules."

The choice to be a sexually active single is life changing and long lasting. In addition to displeasing God and bringing shame to the name of Christ, you expose yourself to the possibility of an unwanted pregnancy, abortion, STDs, and AIDS, not to mention the emotional baggage that goes with opening a box that God wrapped with the words "For Married Couples Only."

Paul in I Corinthians 6:13 says, "The body is not meant for sexual immorality, but for the Lord, and the Lord for the body." I Thessalonians 4:3 says, "It is God's will that you are sanctified, that you abstain from sexual immorality." We should say no to *any* sexual activity outside of marriage. The mandate is the same in all translations of the Bible. God has called us to be holy, holy at all times, including in the 21st century! Imagine being pure and holy in this culture.

We are chosen, and we are royalty. Our bodies house the Holy Spirit. I Corinthians 6:15 says, "Do you not know that your bodies are members of Christ himself? Shall I then take the members of Christ and unite them with a prostitute? Never!" Do you realize

God's indwelled spirit is right there as the third party in any illicit sexual encounter? God would never ask us to do anything that in His power we could not do, but we must have the will to seek God's restraining power in our dating relationships. He can keep us from going too far.

I Corinthians 10:13 says, "No temptation has seized you except what is common to man. And God is faithful; he will not let you be tempted beyond what you can bear. But when you are tempted, he will also provide a way out so that you can stand up under it." God will do His part if we will to do His will. He says we will be tempted. It's a fact of life. But the good news is, as followers of Christ, He promises to empower us to just say, "No!"

I know that we can remain pure. In a society that believes otherwise, I can tell you that it is possible. By God's grace and strength, I have never had sex outside of marriage. I know my boundaries before I go on the first date. I have no regrets about my lifestyle. Have I lost relationships because of my position? Yes, many. Have I cried many nights because of the rejection? Yes. Have I felt weird at times? Lonely? Have I longed to be intimate? Yes. Why did I abstain? Because I love God intensely and want to please Him more than I want to please myself. I treasure my relationship with Him more than a relationship with a man. I don't want to dishonor His name. I believe He knows what is best for me and His best does not include having sex outside of marriage. I'm willing to do it His way or not at all.

A single woman who is serious about pleasing God will have a game plan. She will not put herself in a position to be tempted or to tempt her date. Remember our spirit may be willing, but our flesh is very, very, very, very weak! You just can't trust it. Apostle Paul said, "Put no confidence in the flesh" (Phil. 3:3). We are to make no provisions for allowing the flesh to get out of control. Build in safeguards to keep from yielding to temptation.

If you are saved, you are still human; thus you will be tempted. You will find a man attractive. You will want to touch and have your hands start going south. But boundaries must be set in advance and promises to God must be kept. Remember you never have to disobey God or compromise His principles to get the person He ordained for you. Never! You may yield to your flesh, but never blame God when things don't work out. The Bible says, "Each one is tempted, when by his own evil desire, he is dragged away and enticed" (James 1:14). If you had sex, you did it because you wanted to. You knew Jesus was convicting you when it began to get "hot and heavy." The phone was ringing, the pot was boiling over, you heard a soft voice in your spirit saying, "no, don't do it," but you deliberately ignored all the warning signs, because you wanted to satisfy your flesh.

So what are some possible boundaries? First of all, know yourself. Some women get sexually excited if they simply hold hands with a man. A friend of mine is in this category. She knows herself. For her, holding hands is off limits! It excites her sexually. Likewise, if you know you become "weak in the knees" if you allow a man to come inside your home after a date, then say goodbye at the elevator, at the front door, or in the building lobby. It may be tough, because in all honesty there is a part of you that wishes to end the date in his arms. But as a 1st Class Single, you have resolved that you want to please God more than you want to please your flesh!

That's the kind of resolve Joseph (in the Old Testament) had when his boss' wife attempted to seduce him on a regular basis. He was a hunk and single! He was also a virgin. Every day she harassed him. His response was, I cannot do this thing because it would defile God. He did not make excuses for yielding to temptation. He could have said, *Well, God will understand. After all, I'm a man. I've got testosterone. God knows I need to express myself. Plus, this is a pagan country. When in Rome, do as the Romans do. God is a forgiving God. He understands my dilemma.* No. Without flinching, he refused her advances and left the consequences to God. For sure he faced the wrath of an angry, belligerent, and embarrassed woman! How dare he turn her down, she thought.

After such rejection, Mrs. Potiphar wanted to make sure Joseph paid for the putdown! He was wrongfully accused of rape and sentenced to time behind bars. In prison, he did not blame God or regret his decision. In God's own time, He promoted Joseph from prisoner to prime minister! Only God can pull that off. We honor His Word when we choose to trust and obey and leave the consequences to Him.

Remember: LOVE can wait, but LUST cannot. Beware of locking lips and hips. A good rule to follow is author Elisabeth Elliot's words of advice, "Keep your hands off and your clothes on!" Let's be honest. The longer you date someone you love, the more difficult it is to resist getting physical. It is even more challenging once you are engaged. God knows this and so does our adversary, the devil. His goal is to trip you up by any means necessary! I Peter 5:8-9 reveals how he works and how we can guard ourselves from his attacks: "Be self controlled and alert. Your enemy the devil prowls around like a roaring lion looking for someone to devour. Resist him, standing firm in the faith." James 4:7 says, "Submit yourselves, then to God. Resist the devil, and he will flee from you."

Again, I encourage you to write a list of your boundaries when dating *before* you meet a potential "Mr. Right," and then determine by God's grace to live by them. Pray often. Be honest with God about your sexual temptations. Stay away from dark, cozy places where you will be alone with your date. Plan for temptation. Have an escape route like Joseph did. Remember God will help you, but you can help yourself as well. Stay connected with an accountability partner who can ask you the hard questions about your thought life and your dates. Don't dress provocatively or use sexual innuendo when you talk. Eliminate sexually explicit music, movies, videos, and television shows from your diet. The imagery and sounds are powerful. They are designed to stir your sexual desires.

Some singles may be wondering if there is any hope for those who have already blown it in this department. Perhaps you have not honored God in your dating relationships. You've had sex already or you didn't go all the way, but you went too far for a Christ follower. There is always hope in Christ. I John 1:9 says, "If we confess our sins, He is faithful and just to forgive us of our sins and cleanse us from all unrighteousness."

There is no one perfect walking the earth. We have all sinned in at least one area. That's why we have the Cross. Ask God to forgive you of your past actions and He will. True repentance means to "turn away from." When we truly repent, we are willing to forsake our old ways and allow God to transform our minds. You can begin again. The good news is that you can return to a life of chastity and purity. There is no need to live in condemnation and guilt for your past, once your sins are forgiven! II Corinthians 5:17 says, "Therefore, if anyone is in Christ, he is a new creation; the old has gone, the new has come!"

Rule #17:

Use Your Influence in a Way that Pleases God

God has given you the power of influence as a woman. Do you know that? My mother told me as a teenager, "A man will go as far as *you* let him go." What mother said was right! Again, you can define the relationship and its boundaries. Do you want to conduct yourself in a way that pleases God? Do you want the relationship to be a pleasant memory whether it ends in marriage or not? Do you want to affirm the guy or tear him down? Will he be better off having known you or will he be left in a catatonic state?

We can decide in advance to influence others for

good, to build up or tear down. The Bible says, "Whatever we do in word or deed, do it all in the name of the Lord Jesus" (Col. 3:17). I Corinthians 10:31 says, "Whether you eat or drink, or whatever you do, do it all for the glory of God."

Our motivation in dating should be to please God. Titus admonishes us to consider Christian men as our brothers first. We would not want anyone to abuse, offend, or take advantage of our brothers.

Let's make sure we do not defraud those we are dating. We defraud when we use people, play with their emotions and mislead them for selfish gain. How do you want your date to remember you? Will his testimony be that you were a kind, considerate, and godly woman? Or, will he tell his friends you tried to seduce him? Will he say that you were easy and desperate? Will he think that you have a filthy mouth and a messy house? The choice is yours.

I remember a guy telling me he once dated a Sunday School teacher. He thought she was a committed Christian, but he changed his mind after one memorable date. She suggested they stop by her house on the way to the next event. He says she excused herself, went into the bathroom, and came back out in a red "teddy" ready for action! It's obvious her goal was not to influence him in a way that pleases God.

Rule #18:

Date by the Golden Rule

Many of us learned the Golden Rule as children: "Treat others as you want to be treated." But we have forgotten it as adults. We would want a man to be as caring and tactful as possible if he was breaking up with us. We would want him to be sensitive to our feelings and not tell the world he dumped us. Let's do the same. Be considerate of the other person's feelings. Purpose not to lie or mistreat your date.

Christian dating should look different than non-Christian dating. We should ask ourselves "How would Christ respond in this situation? Would this conversation please Him?" If someone wants to date you but you are not interested, rather than react with a look of disbelief, you can respond graciously and humbly. Living by the Golden Rule means not playing games, especially with someone's emotions. Jesus always left people better off after they met Him. Wouldn't it be great if we could look back on all our dating experiences and know they were pleasant for all involved? We're on our way to accomplishing this if we remember to date by the Golden Rule.

Rule #19:

Consider It a Bad Sign If You Are the Only One Happy About the Relationship

You are a wise person if you are open to the advice of godly parents and friends who love you, know you, and pray for you. Please listen to them. They have nothing to lose except possibly your friendship. If they are willing to put it on the line to share some concerns, be open to what they have to say. Proverbs 19:20 says, "Listen to advice and accept instruction, and in the end you will be wise." Proverbs 27:6 adds, "Wounds from a friend can be trusted."

If you are not dating anyone now, please do yourself a big favor and make a pact that you will be totally transparent and accountable to someone about the next guy you date and really like. Make a promise to seek advice from wise people who know and love you. Seriously consider any feedback they give you. This is one of the ways God uses others to clarify His will.

If you're going down the aisle on your big wedding day, and your mother is crying, your father is in tears, your close friends are crying (and these are not tears of joy), something is seriously wrong with this picture! I believe it's rare that you would be the only person who received the memo from God stating that this is the guy for you, and everybody is wrong except you!

One of my biggest regrets is that I defied my godly mother's concerns and went on with my marriage plans. She is my closest confidante. She is a wise woman who loves God and loves me. She told me that she did not approve of my marriage. She attended the wedding and cried during the ceremony. In the past I had always heeded her advice, but this time I was so sure she was wrong and I was right. I had to be right because it felt so good. We were so compatible. The courtship was God-honoring. My hormones were not moaning; this was NOT a relationship of the flesh. God was first. We talked about what we would do for God. It was the courtship of my dreams. We got along so well, how could this NOT be God?

When my mother expressed some concerns, I

dismissed them, because I felt she believed he wasn't good enough for me. That was the basis of her negativity, I told myself. So what did I do? I began to poll other family members and kept doing so until I found someone who told me what I wanted to hear. That's what we women tend to do. We keep talking to folks until we find someone who affirms and supports our bad decision! Then it's easy to dismiss the naysayers, and justify our actions. Take it from me. Don't do that. You will live to regret it.

God is NOT the author of confusion. Am I saying in EVERY instance you should abandon your plans for marriage, if certain family members don't get on board? Of course not. But I am saying take their concerns seriously. Pray about them. Be open to another point of view and that God could be using the wisdom and counsel of other Christians to reveal that this relationship is not His best. Don't assume that God cannot be against your relationship because it "feels" right and you are so "happy." What is more important: To be "happy" or to be in God's perfect will? Your happiness can turn to sorrow just a few days after you say, "I do." Then you may be haunted with memories of the people who begged you to take it easy and to go slow. Be prayerful. Continue investigating.

The truth is we can be blinded by love. Your true friends will tell you if they think you are settling for second best. But you may not see it because you are just happy to be in a relationship. I remember a friend saying her girlfriends thought her boyfriend was nice, but not of her caliber. She could not see their point until she and the guy broke up. After she started going out with another guy who treated her like royalty, she understood what her friends were saying! She could finally "see" what others had seen all along.

Rule #20:

Don't Marry Potential

Ask yourself, "If he *never* changes, can I live with that?" Secretly, women always want to change men. We consider a man a project. God said to me once, "Cheryl, the Bible says 'Train a child in the way he should go' (Prov. 22:6), it does not say train up a man in the way he should go." I got the message.

Of course, no one is perfect, but when the person has glaring habits you know you can't tolerate, why kid yourself? Who are *you* to try to change another adult to make your life more comfortable? Would you want someone seeing you as a project? That sounds like the job of the Holy Spirit who has the power to conform us into the image of Christ. Don't try to be "Holy Spirit, Jr."

Instead, pray for your man; talk to your man, but accept this truth about your man: what you see is what you get! And sometimes what you don't see, is what you get! Accept him as he is, then decide whether you can live with that. But be careful not to make compromises in desperation. You will be happier by accepting your man as he is. Later, he may change because He wants to, not because he has to.

Rule #21:

Don't Go Down the Aisle If You Aren't at Perfect Peace

When in doubt, don't. Wait. Keep praying until you hear from God and experience "His peace that passeth all understanding" (Phil. 4:7). The Bible says, "Let the peace of Christ rule in your hearts" (Col. 3:15). God's direction always brings with it a divine peace. Psalm 34:14 says, "Seek peace and pursue it." God speaks to us through our spirits. He speaks in a still small voice. When we experience God's peace, it doesn't mean everything will add up and you will have all the answers. But it does mean that you are confident that you are moving at God's direction, and that your decision is not of your own choosing.

We have to be careful not to attempt to "conjure" up or manufacture this peace to justify going after someone we want. We can easily dismiss any uneasiness or doubt or questions about the person, because we want him! God is trying to get through to us, but we put up major blockage. We are stubborn. We don't want to entertain any possibility that this relationship may not be God's best for us. Why? Because we think it is, and that's all that matters to us at the moment.

But when we really want God's input, all we have to do is ask. That's what Proverbs 3:6 says: "In all thy ways acknowledge Him, and He will direct our paths." God wants us to make the right decision and He wants us to be guided by His peace. Why is this so important? Life is tough. Life is full of challenges, especially when it comes to marriage between two flawed, sinful individuals.

This journey can be more difficult if we are plagued daily by this thought: "God didn't tell me to marry him; that's why we're having so many problems. I did not have the peace of God before I went down the aisle." But when you have peace and confidence before marriage that you are in the will of God, you can rely on that knowledge and face your trials confidently, knowing that God will see you through and that He will give you wisdom regarding how to be a good wife, and how to make the most of your marriage. If you are genuinely at peace from the get-go, then no matter how difficult it may become, you are never plagued with thoughts that you are out of the will of God. So, once again, do not say, "I Do" unless God has said "I ordain and bless this union."

Rule #22:

Study the Ingredients of a Great Marriage

Many marriages are shipwrecked. Others are barely surviving. Unfortunately, the divorce rate for Christians is just as high as it is for the general population.

The good news is that there are some good marriages, some happily married couples! Study these thriving marriages. Find out why they are successful. Befriend these couples. Ask if you can spend time with them. Query them on what makes their marriage work. Ask if they can be your mentors. You will learn a lot by closely observing them.

I've had the privilege twice in my life to live in the homes of couples who have enduring, strong, and loving marriages. I learned so much by quietly observing how they respected each other, and demonstrated love and kindness to each other. They allowed me to ask questions about their relationships. This time was extremely invaluable. I began to formulate my ideas about what makes a marriage work.

Do your homework and learn from the best marriages. Read books about building a successful relationship. Attend seminars on building healthy relationships. Once you get engaged, sign up for premarital counseling. Always keep in mind that you are only one half of the equation. You cannot have a successful relationship unless your mate is just as committed to reaching the same goal. Otherwise, you'll be constantly frustrated trying to get him to go somewhere he does not want to go, and to be someone he does not want to be.

Rule #23:

Remember, Marriage is Not a Better State, Just Another State

Many singles think they have not arrived unless they cross over to the "other side." I know it's one thing to be single in your early 20s, but another to be single when you are in your late 20s, 30s, or 40s, and have yet to entertain a serious marriage proposal. Sure, your biological clock is ticking. But remember, from God's perspective, marriage is not a better season, just another season. In nature, we have four seasons: fall, winter, spring and summer. Each is different. We typically look forward to each for what it offers. We don't expect 90-degree weather in the winter. We don't look for snow in the summer. We may prefer one season to another, but we realize the need for all.

We may prefer marriage (or think we do), but singleness is the gift God has given us now. Singleness is not second rate to marriage. There are certain liberties and freedoms you have as a 1st Class Single. Think of the successful singles in the Bible. Jesus, John the Baptist, and Daniel never married. God used Joseph and David mightily during their single years. Ruth and the prophetess Anna served God faithfully as widows. God wastes nothing. He wants us to fully enjoy this season and not think we are wasting away until Mr. Right comes along!

Rule #24:

Be Real. Be Who You Are!

So many couples are perpetrating when they are dating. As my brother Jerry says all the time, "dating is designed to conceal, not reveal." Couples are afraid to be themselves because they fear rejection. You can only fake it for so long. Don't try to impress your date. When you are no longer true to yourself in a relationship, that's a pretty good indicator that this person is not for you. I've known women who compromise on their preferences and are eventually disgusted with themselves and their choices.

Of course, there is some compromise in navigating a friendship, but when you totally abandon your true self in hopes of nabbing a guy, you are the main loser in the long run. Refrain from embellishing your "resume." Don't try to be something you are not. Don't act as if you're smarter than you are, have more money than you do or are more confident than you really are. Don't name drop. Just be you.

Again, the person God has for you will accept you, warts and all! We all have flaws. No one is perfect. It's comforting to know that you will not miss God's best for you because of your looks, size, background, and ethnicity, etc. Some women are perpetually depressed because they believe they are still single due to their physical attributes. They constantly say "if only..." They say to themselves, "if only I were younger, smarter, prettier, thinner." All they have to do is look around. They will see all kinds of married women: short, tall, thin, heavy, poor, wealthy. You name it!

The answer for all women is to blossom into the beautiful flower and fragrance God deemed us to be. Let's accept ourselves 100 percent. It's refreshing when we are free to be ourselves. It's a sign we are at peace with how God made us. He never makes mistakes.

The Bible says, "Woe unto him that striveth with his Maker. Shall the clay say to him that fashioneth it, what makest thou" (Isaiah 45:9)? "You are fearfully and wonderfully made" (Psalm 139:14). Meditate on those words for a moment and let them sink in, especially the phrase, "wonderfully made." Yes, you were wonderfully made by the Creator of the universe who does all things with excellence. God was pleased when He made you just as you are. When we question our looks and our abilities, it's so important to stop and meditate on the creativity of a sovereign God and His concept of beauty.

Now, being the "real you" does not mean you are content with attitudes and actions you know are displeasing to God. We should all be striving to become more Christ-like and to make the most of the "package" He's given us. That's all we can do: to make the most of what we have and the least of what we don't have. We need to cooperate with God's work of conforming us into His image. But beyond that, we are all wired differently, with different temperaments, preferences, goals, looks, and desires.

I realize it's not always easy to accept yourself. It has taken me most of my life to be comfortable with just being me, the unique person God made me to be. I grew up with seven brothers and no sisters, so I was a tomboy. They played with toy guns, so I rejected dolls and played with guns. I haven't always liked my looks or personality. For years, I wanted to look like someone else, and have a more docile personality. I compared myself to others. I judged myself by their looks and talents. This was a dangerous habit.

The Bible says, " For we dare not make ourselves of the number or compare ourselves with some that commend themselves, they are not wise" (II Cor. 10:12). When we are obsessed with comparing, we can exhibit either pride or arrogance because in our minds we are prettier or smarter. On the other hand, if we believe another woman is prettier or smarter than we are, we can develop an inferiority complex and depression follows. Either attitude is wrong. Comparing is insidious and an unwise use of time. There will always be someone more gifted, talented or beautiful. So what! Their "package" will not impact your assignment.

I remember a time when I was obsessed with comparing my performance and wardrobe as a news anchor/host to other women on television. I will never forget one Saturday morning while praying, the Lord spoke to my heart and said, "It's OK for you to admire other women who are successful television anchors, but it's wrong for you to emulate them. I want you to concentrate on being the woman I created you to be. I put something special down in you and I want you to concentrate on bringing that forward and being the 'best you that you can be'."

I have never forgotten that revelation. That message wasn't just for me but for every person. God has uniquely gifted you to accomplish in life what only you can do. No one can do it quite like you.

God loves diversity. Just look at the earth and all the different fruits, trees, plants, animals, etc. Whenever I enter a grocery store, I love to take a panoramic view of the great selection of fruits and vegetables. There are so many different colors, tastes, and sizes. When I eat fruit, for example, I never compare a strawberry to an orange, apple or pear. I don't expect it to taste like them. I simply savor the great taste for what it is, a strawberry. I enjoy the variety of fruits for their distinct flavors. That's what God intended by making us different.

So, why is it so difficult for us as women to revel in our uniqueness? Why do we need to compare our looks and our abilities to those of another woman?

Why do we feel inferior because we're different? These feelings are not of God. We are to fully embrace how He made and gifted us for His glory. When we understand this, we will not feel the need to be anyone but who the Designer intended us to be.

Many times, if we don't suffer from comparison, we instead revel in competing with other women. We must also resist this temptation. This spirit of competition can stifle and ruin friendships. Inwardly, we are sometimes jealous, envious, and covetous of another woman's good fortune. We resent the praise she receives. We believe *we* deserve it.

How is the spirit of competition expressed? Let's say someone praises your friend. Instead of smiling and nodding in agreement, you find something wrong with her, anything, and point it out. Are you genuinely happy when your girlfriend gets a higher paying job, a promotion, or a wonderful husband? Or do you believe you deserve all these things more than she does? If so, this attitude reveals a serious "heart" ailment that is in desperate need of surgery. I've had to go under the knife of the Holy Spirit after He revealed a spirit of competition and comparison with some of my closest friends. I hate to admit that there have been times I was consumed with comparison, and a quiet spirit of competition. God turned his searchlight on me and revealed these attitudes were wrong and displeasing to Him. "The heart is desperately wicked," Jeremiah 17:9 says, and it is.

To combat these feelings, we must admit them and ask God to deliver us from every ounce of comparison and unhealthy competition. Whenever I sense just a twinge of jealousy or insecurity, I immediately pray and ask God to purge me of these "diseases." I pray to be genuinely happy for the successes of others. I regularly take my spiritual "pulse" if I find myself "name dropping" or "putting down" someone to make myself look good. I know these actions are symptoms that there is something terribly wrong with me: There is a shortage of genuine love. Fortunately, we can go to our Savior for help, and He promises to always answer. Every time I've taken my shortcomings to God, He has always healed me of the maladies.

When I think of comparison or competition, three Bible stories come to mind. In John 21, Jesus tells Peter how he will die. Peter is initially excited since he will be a martyr for the cause of Christ. But immediately he looks over at John (the disciple whom Christ loves) and asks Jesus, what's going to happen to John. Peter was not content with his assignment. He wanted to know how it measured up to John's outcome. Jesus used the direct approach and told Peter, "If I want him to remain alive until I return, what is that to you? You must follow me" (John 21:22). I believe Peter got the message: *Mind your own business and be busy fulfilling My purposes for you. Don't worry about anyone else's assignment.*

The friendships between Jonathan and David in the Old Testament and Mary and her cousin Elisabeth in the New Testament are wonderful models of relationships, free from competition and comparison. Jonathan, King Saul's son, was in line to be the next King of Israel. But God had chosen an obscure shepherd boy, David, to be the next king. Jonathan was not jealous or covetous of David. In fact, he loved him as a brother. Jonathan did everything he could to protect David from his jealous father who wanted to kill him. Instead of resenting David, he embraced him. He recognized the sovereignty of God at work and relinquished any sense of entitlement he had to the throne. Where true love flourishes, there is no room for jealousy or envy, comparing or competing.

I love the account in Luke 1 of Mary opting to stay with her much older cousin, Elisabeth, for three months after an angel told her what appeared to be the impossible. The Virgin Mary would become the mother of Jesus and the barren Elisabeth was pregnant in her old age. When Mary arrived at Elisabeth's home, Elisabeth called *her* blessed, and in a spirit of humility said, "Why is this granted to me, that the mother of my Lord should come to me?" Elisabeth did not compare her pregnancy or position to that of Mary's. She did not question God about why He chose Mary over her to bear the Son of God. Elisabeth was older, wiser, and had been faithful to God longer. She had fiercely desired a child for years. Mary was unmarried. Still, Elisabeth didn't think, "Lord, this is so unfair for her to get this prominent position that she doesn't deserve!" There was no conceit in Elisabeth's heart. She had only humility and sheer joy for the both of them. She allowed God to be God.

I believe this was a relationship of mutual love and respect because Mary would not have quickly gone to Elisabeth's home and stayed there so long if there was a spirit of envy and rivalry. We can tell when someone is not happy about our good fortune. We can sense when a friend doesn't think we deserve that promotion and is envious of us. When we detect such negative vibes, we usually withdraw and are reluctant to share our joy.

I'm sure Mary felt free to talk and dream with Elisabeth and to get wise counsel. Why? Both accepted their assignments from God, and were grateful for His kindness. Elisabeth possessed true humility. She did not think any higher of herself than she ought. She had the proper perspective that "every good and perfect gift is from above" (James 1:17). She had a thankful heart.

When we possess the same attitude as Elisabeth and Mary, we are free to sincerely applaud the successes of others, and know that by doing so we take nothing away from God's divine plan for us. I pray often to possess an "Elisabeth" spirit. I desire to follow in her footsteps with no malice, envy, or jealousy in my heart for anyone, no matter what wonderful and desirable blessings God is showering on them.

Rule #25:

Know Your Worth!

Carry yourself with dignity and respect. Don't let a man walk over you. Know your worth, and act accordingly. Remember you are the prize! A man obtains favor from God when *he* finds a wife. If you are striving to be a woman of virtue, Proverbs 31:10 says, "Your price is far above rubies." Don't sell yourself cheap! From God's perspective, you are a precious jewel.

I firmly believe that Christian women should be the most confident women walking the earth. Why? God is our Father, we are royalty, and we have access to all His riches on an as-needed basis.

When you know your worth, you walk with confidence. You won't settle for someone trying to get you at below market price. If you owned a Rolls Royce and you decided to sell it, you would not accept an offer of $10,000 for this luxury car. You would be insulted. Why? You know the worth of this car and you are no fool! If you had to keep it on the market for a year or more, you would do so, rather than accept a ridiculously low price. You may make some compromises, especially if you overpriced the car to begin with, but you are not going to give the car away at a rock bottom price.

Well, how many women have played themselves cheap just to get a guy? They neither ask for nor expect anything of him. They are willing to support him, cover all his expenses, move him into their homes, and give him sex just so they can say they finally got a "man." They're right. All they got was a "man." They got some flesh. That's about all they got—some male flesh. Not a husband, not a provider, not a spiritual leader, just a "man."

A single Christian woman who knows her worth is not desperate. She is calm because she trusts God. She is free to fully develop all her gifts and abilities, and strives to be the woman God wants her to be. She is confident she will not have to lower her standards to get Mr. Right.

I often think of the story of Amanda Smith, a slave born in 1837. She became a famous missionary evangelist, preaching in England and Africa. Her story is told in the book "Great Women of the Christian Faith." Once, when she stood before women of wealth to sing with her beautiful voice, she suddenly realized that she was only a washwoman, and she became afraid to sing. Then she remembered, "I belong to royalty, and am well acquainted with the king of kings, and am better known and better understood among the great family above than I am on earth."[1] She went on to sing boldly and beautifully. So, never forget your high ranking and expensive price tag!

Rule #26:

Concentrate More on Inner than Outer Beauty

No matter how beautiful you are, over time, your looks will fade. Face lifts, liposuction, botox, and exercise will help you look younger, but you will still get old, and begin to look older. Proverbs 31:30 says, "Charm is deceitful and beauty is vain. But the woman who fears the Lord shall be praised." God cares about inner beauty that does not fade not beauty of the flesh.

Our society worships the body. Women spend billions of dollars a year on beauty products. It's so important to us to look good and feel good. There is nothing wrong with wanting to look our best, but we are not to be obsessed with our outward appearance. We should instead be consumed with developing Christ-like character, a servant's heart, and a meek and quiet spirit. I Peter 3:3 gives timely advice to women. "Let not your adorning be of expensive clothes but instead let it be that of a calm and teachable spirit. This kind of beauty will not fade."

Why not spend your time on a beauty regimen that God says will make you a true beauty in His sight? Take inventory of your inner appearance. Are you kind, gentle, gracious, confident, teachable, thoughtful, hospitable, affirming, humble, tenderhearted, disciplined, and godly in all you do, think, and say? A daily workout regimen for shaping up in these areas will count for Eternity. These traits will make you more attractive to a potential marriage partner and to others as well. A man may be initially attracted to you physically, but these inner characteristics can keep him attracted to you for life.

What does Peter mean when he says that a woman's adornment should be that of the inner self, the unfading beauty of a gentle and quiet spirit? A gentle or meek woman is poised with strength under control. The Master controls her power. For example, such a woman has the vocabulary to tell you off, to give you a "piece of her mind" (in Jesus' name) but she doesn't. An article I once read in "Discipleship Journal" said, "The Greek word for 'meek' was commonly used to describe a wild animal that had been trained, tamed and otherwise harnessed…Once broken, a good horse doesn't require much correction. He has learned to accept the reins of his master and a gentle tug is all that is needed to urge him one direction or another."[1]

A woman who has placed the reins of her life in the guiding hand of the Master may give up control. A meek woman is humble and gentle. She shows patience with others and herself. She is teachable, open for correction and possesses a willingness to be instructed. She is not a know-it-all who thinks, "Who does *she* think *she* is to tell me this?"

A woman with a calm (quiet) spirit is not easily vexed. She can remain calm despite her circumstances, because she trusts God totally. It doesn't mean she's a woman who never talks or has an opinion. Neither does it mean she's a doormat. But she is not easily agitated. She is not afraid of her future, because her hope and trust are in a God who always does what is right and just.

Paul encouraged women in I Timothy 2:9-10 to "adorn yourself with godliness and good works." What are you known for? The latest fashions or your familiarity with Scriptures? Your gorgeous hairstyle or your good works in the church and community? Your looks or your love for God?

A 1st Class Single will pursue inner beauty over outer beauty. There are women who spend no less than two hours a day at the gym firming and toning their bodies. That's wonderful, but how many women are just as committed to spending at least an hour a day working on their inner beauty with prayer, meditation, worship, Bible study, and memorizing Scripture? God teaches that of the two, inner beauty is the most important.

Rule #27:

Make the Most of Your Singleness

Do you realize your singleness is a gift? I know you may answer: "No, let this gift pass me by. I want a man. I don't want to be single. I want to be a wife!" But you know every gift from God is good. Make the most of your singleness. Accept it. Embrace it. Why not maximize this season for God's glory?

There are specific things He wants you to learn, develop, and do. There are places He wants you to go, and people's lives He wants you to impact. Why waste this season focusing on what you don't have when you could be making the most of this opportunity? I'm embarrassed to think how much precious time I've lost over the years dreaming and longing for a loving relationship.

Live in the present, not in the future. Seize every opportunity, because tomorrow is not promised. Find out what God wants you to do today. Let's say you are 25 years old and you can buy a house, but you refuse to because your dream is to buy your first house with your mate. What you don't realize is, you may not meet your future mate until you are 38! Look at all the unfruitful time. You have 13 years to live in your own home, be a wise steward of your money, and be in a better position to buy a nicer home (if you want to) when Mr. Right comes along! In Ephesians 5:15-17 we are told: "Be very careful, then, how you live—not as unwise but as wise, making the most of every opportunity, because the days are evil. Therefore do not be foolish, but understand what the Lord's will is."

Use this time to fully develop your gifts and your intimacy with God. In I Corinthians 7, Paul says, the single person can freely pursue one purpose: undivided devotion to God. When you're single, you only have to please one person, Jesus Christ! Ask God how He wants you to glorify Him in this season of your life. Does He want you to get that degree? Go on the mission field? Start a business? Mentor a child? The possibilities for 1st Class Singles are awesome. Pursue them with great vigor.

Be busy in your calling and in your area of giftedness. Take an inventory of yourself. What are your strengths physically, intellectually, emotionally, spiritually, and vocationally? Capitalize on them. Fully develop and nourish them. What do you want to change? What do you want to do? Make a list. And, please remember that you can change your weight, but not your height, so don't focus on what you cannot change. Unfortunately, we spend too much time doing just that, majoring in the minors and minoring in the majors! Do you want to travel the world? Learn the fine art of entertaining? Now is the time to do it. God wants us to live life to the fullest!

Rule #28:

Be Friendly

I know this one sounds so simple, but ask yourself and others for their opinion. Ask them straight up: "Am I friendly? Am I nice?" Their answers may surprise you. Proverbs 18:24 says, "A man who has friends, must himself be friendly." Are you approachable? Do you reach out and take the initiative to meet people? Typically, the women who meet men are those who are friendly. One of my girlfriends has never had a problem meeting men, because she is so warm and outgoing. She always speaks to people anywhere and everywhere—at the airport, in the supermarket, and at the gas station. Some men can be intimidated or nervous about approaching a group of women or a woman by herself. But if her body language and her face say "it's OK to approach me," he is more comfortable in taking that chance. I heard someone say, "There is never a reason to be unkind."

It could be you are not interested in the guy, but you can still be nice. He might introduce you to his brother or best friend who you may like! You never know where an act of kindness will lead. Remember Rebekah's kindness to a servant led to meeting and marrying wealthy Isaac!

Rule #29:

Cultivate "Sister" Friendships

It is so important to cultivate friendships with like-minded women. Be deliberate when choosing your close friends. They will rub off on you. Proverbs 27:17 says, "As iron sharpens iron, so one man (or woman) sharpens another." I'm convinced that if we are to be the women God truly called us to be, we will reach our goal with the help of other women. I can speak from personal experience that God has been faithful to bring women into my life to help get me where He wanted me to go, to help develop, encourage, and mentor me.

One woman I met during my college years allowed me to live in her home for a year. I learned much about entertaining, being organized, being hospitable, and cultivating a successful marriage.

I have news anchor friends who helped me develop a flair for fashion and taught me how to apply my own makeup for television. They encouraged me in my career and gave me job leads.

In Titus, chapter 2, older women are admonished to teach younger women. Each one of us is an "older" woman to someone younger. My mother, my No. 1 confidante, has always been my role model of what a godly woman looks like. She loves God intensely, is a prayer warrior, and always does what pleases God, even if it hurts. Over the years, I've gleaned much from her wisdom and it has kept me from making many decisions that would have been detrimental to my well being. We all need each other. No woman is an island. We need the counsel and perspective of God-fearing women. Look at the mentoring relationships of Naomi and Ruth. Ruth listened and followed Naomi's advice on how to get a man (a rich one at that!), Boaz.

If you don't have healthy relationships like these in your life, ask God to bring the right women across your path so you can be a blessing to each other. These friendships are invaluable.

Rule #30:

Refuse to Live in the Past

Let's say you've messed up big time in past relationships. You've blown it. You've made all the wrong moves. You've lost your self-esteem and your virginity in the process. You are ashamed of your actions. You chose to abort that child. Perhaps you've aborted more than one child. You are laden with guilt. You are struggling with past failure and can't seem to move forward. This rule is especially for you. Refuse to live in the past. Instead rehearse what you know about God, seek His forgiveness, and renew your mind daily. God can still use you. He still has great plans for your life. The race is not over, so don't get sidelined by your mistakes.

Satan, our adversary, would love nothing more than for you to wallow in self-pity and lick your wounds. He can bombard your mind daily with thoughts that you are all washed up and beyond the realm of God's use. I know because that's what He told me on a daily basis when my husband left me. I will never forget that dreary season of my life. There were days I did not want to get out of bed. I did not look forward to the day. Satan barraged my mind with thoughts such as: "God can never use you again. Your testimony is shot. You have messed up big time!" I heard this over and over again. It was an intense battle for my mind.

I know these thoughts were not of God, because the Bible says, "There is therefore now no condemnation to those who are in Christ Jesus" (Romans 8:1). God is not the author of a spirit of condemnation. I had to rehearse what I knew about God: He is a just and righteous judge who knows all the facts. My heartbreak did not catch Him by surprise because He knows all things. Romans 8:28 is true: "All things work together for good, to those who love Him and to those who are called according to His purpose." I knew I loved God with all my heart, so I embraced His Word, asked for His forgiveness, and chose to renew my mind with His thoughts, not mine.

I began to listen to what He wanted to teach me through this ordeal. Sure enough, there were major lessons to be learned. First, I was told to put my "spiritual" pride on the altar and walk in humility. I had been a know-it-all, smug Christian, who resembled a Pharisee (you know the religious sect Jesus was always putting in its place). Of course, I did not see this side of me, until "my man" left. I was determined to have a perfect, Exhibit A marriage by hook or by crook. Thankfully I listened when God told me to stop worrying about "my Christian reputation."

Second, He took me to Romans 8:29, a verse I had not focused on. It says that God's assignment is to "conform us to His image," by any means necessary. I was seeking happiness. He was looking for holiness; to make me fit for heaven. I share this to encourage you that God can use what you offer to Him. As author Elisabeth Elliot often says, "Every situation, if offered to God, can be your gateway to joy." Offer Him your pain, your disappointment, your disillusionment, your betrayal. Take it to the foot of the Cross and leave it there.

One Sunday when I was going through my ordeal and was in church service, that's what I heard the Lord say to me: "Bring it all to *Me* and leave it at the foot of the Cross." Jesus said, "Cheryl, that's why I died. Not just for your salvation, but for every pain, every disappointment, every sin, past, present, and future." That's what the Cross symbolizes. Right then, I offered Him everything. I was cleansed and set free! That spirit of depression left. I was no longer paralyzed by my past. I had given it to the Savior of the world. You can do the same. He is no respecter of persons.

One thing I love about reading the Bible is that it is candid about its heroes, revealing the good, the bad, and the ugly. King David, for instance, was known as a man after God's own heart, yet he sinned big time. He not only committed adultery with Bathsheba, but he plotted the battlefield death of her husband once he found out Bathsheba got pregnant from their illicit encounter. But the story does not end there. When David was confronted about his adulterous act by Nathan the prophet, he owned up to it. He had every reason to be depressed for the rest of his life, but instead he chose to cry out to God for forgiveness and to repent of his sin. God forgave him and cleansed him of all his unrighteousness. He promises to do the same when we sincerely seek forgiveness.

Man may not forget our mistakes but God does not hold them against us, though we may face consequences as a result of our disobedience. In David's case, the child died. But God is merciful and full of grace no matter the sin. He chose Solomon as the next king of Israel. He was David's second son by Bathsheba. Why did God pick Solomon? He could have chosen an heir from David's sons by his other wives, but no, he chose Solomon. I believe he was saying to David, *This is proof I have forgiven you. I will exalt this seed.*

Peter in the New Testament also failed God. He had walked with Jesus for three years, yet when pressed, he denied Jesus three times. He even cursed! Peter refused to wallow in self-pity. Instead he cried out for forgiveness. He received it. Jesus already knew what Peter was going to do and had prayed for him, that his faith would not fail. He did not pray that Peter would not fail, but that his faith would not fail.

Do you still have faith after your failure? God can use you! God used Peter mightily on the Day of Pentecost. What if he had been still riddled with depression, hiding in a back room, and refusing to move forward because of his denial? When God forgives us, we are forgiven forever! That is why it is so important, in an attitude of humility, to own up to your sins or mistakes, open your heart to God's cleansing and forgiveness, move forward, and daily renew your mind with God's Word. Philippians 4:8 says, "Whatever is true, whatever is noble, whatever is right, whatever is pure, whatever is lovely, whatever is admirable—if anything is excellent or praiseworthy—think about such things."

Conclusion

The words of F. W. Robertson in my favorite devotional offer encouragement along the journey: "It is not by regretting what is irreparable that true work is to be done, but by making the best of what we are…Life, like war, is a series of mistakes, and he is not the best Christian nor the best general who makes the fewest false steps. He is the best who wins the most splendid victories by the retrieval of mistakes. Forget mistakes; organize victory out of mistakes!"[1]

That is what I've attempted to do in writing *1st Class Single*: retrieve my dating mistakes and turn them into victories for other singles. None of us can change our past, but we can learn from it and be wiser.

May you refer to the rules in *1st Class Single* whenever you need a refresher course or you meet someone new on the horizon. The ultimate fulfilling pursuit of a 1st Class Single woman will always be to do what honors God.

For More Information

Cheryl Martin is available for conferences, seminars, and other speaking engagements. She speaks on a variety of topics related to career advancement, purpose, relationships, self-esteem, and personal motivation.

Prior to joining BET in 1992, Cheryl worked as a reporter and producer for various stations in Washington, DC, including the NBC owned station and the ABC affiliate. She graduated from Northwestern University with a B.S. in Speech (Radio-TV) and a M.S. in Journalism (Broadcast).

To contact Cheryl regarding speaking at your event or to order products, including an autographed copy of this book, audiocassettes, and compact discs, please visit her website or write:

www.cherylmartin.org

OR

Cheryl Martin
P.O. Box 15285
Chevy Chase, MD 20825

Notes

Rule #1: Pursue God, Not a Guy!

1. Psalm 26:3; 27:4-5; 63:1-3,6-8

Rule #3: Want God's Will, Not Your Way

1. John 4:34; 5:30; 6:38; 8:28, 8:50, 8:54

Rule #7: Create a Marriage Resume and Classified Ad

1. Neil Clark Warren, *Two Dates or Less* (Nashville: Thomas Nelson, 1999), Chapter 3, pp. 45-58.

Rule #25: Know Your Worth!

1. Edith Deen, *Great Women of the Christian Faith* (Uhrichsville: Barbour, 1959), p. 236.

Rule #26: Concentrate More on Inner Beauty Than Outer Beauty

1. Matt T. Friedman, "Is Meekness Weakness?" *Discipleship Journal* (Issue 45, 1998): p. 19.

Conclusion

1. Mary W. Tileston, *Daily Strength for Daily Needs* (Public Domain), December 31, F. W. Robertson.

Printed in the United States
69831LV00002B/262-309

9 781591 605690